The Gift of Presence

The Gift of Presence

A Guide to Helping
Those Who Suffer

Joe E. Pennel, Jr.

ABINGDON PRESS
Nashville, Tennessee

THE GIFT OF PRESENCE
A GUIDE TO HELPING THOSE WHO SUFFER

Copyright © 2009 by Abingdon Press

This book is printed on acid-free paper.

Library of Congress Cataloging-in-Publication Data

Pennel, Joe E.
   The gift of presence : a guide to helping those who suffer / Joseph E. Pennel, Jr.
      p. cm.
   Includes bibliographical references.
   ISBN 978-1-4267-0214-3 (pbk. : alk. paper)
   1. Church work. 2. Suffering—Religious aspects—Christianity. 3. Helping behavior—Religious aspects—Christianity. 4. Caring—Religious aspects—Christianity. I. Title.
   BV4335.P45 2009
   253--dc22
                                        2009008725

09 10 11 12 13 14 15 16 17 18—10 9 8 7 6 5 4 3 2 1

MANUFACTURED IN CHINA

To
Janene, Melanie, Larry, Heather, Keith

For
those who suffer and cannot hide their pain

CONTENTS

INTRODUCTION

My vocation as a pastor has drawn me to writing this book. For over forty years I have stood beside those who suffer. I have seen people suffer as a result of illness, broken relationships, moral failure, the loss of a loved one, and the loss of income. These experiences have caused me to reflect on the meaning of suffering in both theoretical and practical ways. The aim of this book is to provide practical yet substantive help for anyone desiring to reach out to family, friends, and strangers who are caught in the tangle of suffering.

Suffering is a universal theme that joins people at every point on earth. In a strange and mystical way, it makes us aware of our transcendence and destines us to go beyond ourselves. It happens, as we know, at different moments on the path of life. It takes place in various and different ways. It assumes different dimensions. It evokes either compassion or despair. It consoles or it intimidates. It is tangible with an intangible meaning. It leads to either joy or despair. Yet one thing is certain: Suffering is inseparable from the life of humanity.

It is my hope that *The Gift of Presence* will be a treasure for those who want to better understand suffering; who desire to know what to say and not to say, and what to do and not to do; and who seek practical resources that will enable them to be truly present with those in need.

Ministering to those who are suffering does not mean that we understand all there is to know about suffering or have all the "answers," because suffering is, at best, an intangible mystery. It simply means that we are present to those who suffer so that they might not suffer alone. This handbook provides practical suggestions for those who care enough to walk alongside those who are traveling the winding path of suffering. It also provides help for understanding the different responses individuals can have to suffering and addresses some common questions they often have about God during such an experience by reaching out in practical and compassionate ways.

We offer those who are suffering a sacred gift when we agree to be present to their pain. Being with them in meaningful ways can provide a source of safety and comfort.

It also is a gift to us because it is in such moments that we experience the holy.

Robert Browning Hamilton's poem "Along the Road" tells of walking a mile with Pleasure and learning nothing despite her constant chatter. In contrast, when he walks with silent Sorrow, he learns many things. As we assist those who are suffering, we also learn something of great value for the living of these days.

PART 1

Reaching Out to Those Who Suffer

The gift of presence is rooted in the belief that the living Christ is present with us and with those who suffer. Those who desire to give and help need simply to bear witness to the Christ who is already present.

CHAPTER 1

Following the Example of the Good Samaritan

The teachings of Jesus encourage us to reach out to those who suffer. For example, the parable of the good Samaritan has a word for us about how a follower of Christ should respond to those who are caught in the web of suffering. The story goes like this:

"A man was going down from Jerusalem to Jericho, and fell into the hands of robbers, who stripped him, beat him, and went away, leaving him half dead. Now by chance a priest was going down that road; and when he saw him, he passed by on the other side. So likewise a Levite, when he came to the place and saw him, passed by on the other side. But a Samaritan while traveling came near him; and when he saw him, he was moved with pity. He went to him and bandaged his wounds, having poured oil and wine on them. Then he put him on his own animal, brought him to an inn, and took care of him. The next day he took out two denarii, gave them to the innkeeper, and said, 'Take care of him; and when I come back, I will repay you whatever more you spend.' Which of these three, do you think, was a neighbor to the man who fell into the hands of the robbers?" [The man answered Jesus], "The one who showed him mercy." Jesus said to him, "Go and do likewise." *(Luke 10:30-37)*

This parable of Jesus vividly reminds us that the Gospel does not give us permission to pass by on the other side as did the priest and the Levite. The story beckons us to stop by and care for those who are wounded and broken down by life.

Becoming a "Good Samaritan"

Consider how we become the good Samaritan each and every time we turn to those who are suffering. The title "good Samaritan" fits every person who is moved by the misfortune of another. It is far more than having a casual curiosity about another's pain. It is the heart moving toward availability.

The indwelling Christ does not make our hearts cold toward those who are torn by the bite of suffering. The reverse is true. The more we are open to the living Christ, the more we will have a hunger to reach out to those who are beaten down by life.

It is worth noting that the Samaritan does not remain detached from the man who has been beaten and robbed. He does not limit his response to merely feeling sorry for the one who has been injured. He is moved to offer tangible help to the man who was half dead. So, a good Samaritan is anyone who offers the kind of embodied help that flows from a heart that is filled with the love of Christ. It is the kind of help that carries a price tag. It costs something.

If we are to reach out to those who are impaired by suffering, we must have the will to do so. If we are turned in upon ourselves, we will have great difficulty in giving ourselves to the needs of others.

It is here that we are put in touch with one of the key teachings of the Christian faith: We cannot have fruitful and meaningful lives without reaching out to those who walk the road of suffering. Likewise, we cannot truly find ourselves until we are willing and able to give ourselves to others.

Suffering also has the strange power to unleash love. This happens in two ways. First, when we suffer, we are more in tune with the suffering of others, which opens us to respond with compassionate love.

For example, a few years ago I developed a strange but real travel anxiety. I had traveled widely in both the United States and many parts of the world, and I had never felt anxious while traveling. On one occasion we were on a ship, and I put one of those motion sickness patches behind my ears. Without knowing what was happening, I suddenly had a physical reaction to the chemicals. I started perspiring, and I had a severe discomfort in my chest. My mind jumped to the conclusion that I was having a heart attack while we were in a very remote area off the coast of Alaska. To say that I was frightened would be to minimize the entire episode.

When we arrived home, I went to my physician and discovered that people do react to these patches in strange ways. However, this information did not wipe out my anxiety about future ventures. The same feelings were triggered each and every time we were away from home. The experience was so severe that I had to turn to professional help. I am happy to say that drug therapy, self-talk, and meditation have contributed to solving ninety percent of my problems with travel.

My suffering with anticipatory travel anxiety has given me an instant connection with persons who have had similar experiences. I am also more compassionate toward those who have walked the same path. Because of my experiences, it is more natural for me to reach out to such individuals with empathy and compassion.

Second, suffering calls us to respond with unselfish human love. Some people answer that call and some do not, but the call is still present. A good Samaritan will not, with indifference, pass by the suffering of another person. Whether in major or minor ways, a good Samaritan has a helpful and powerful solidarity with those who suffer in either major or minor ways; and he or she cannot and will not withhold love from those who are in need.

Organized Responses to Suffering

Let us not forget that there are times when the many responses to suffering need to be organized so that more comprehensive help can be given. We see this with physicians, nurses, clinics, hospitals, counselors, congregational care groups, and clergy. I call these "good Samaritan" organizations, and we need each of them in a rather crucial way. It is important for us to find many ways to offer gratitude and encouragement to those whose lives are spent in reaching out to broken people.

Also, we must not forget the importance of having many webs of caring. Many of these groups are woven into the fabric of congregational life. We see this voluntary work in Stephen Ministers, lay hospital visitation, prayer groups, and various networks of caring. Larger tasks require careful organization, and we should be grateful to those who care enough to order the life of the congregation around the needs of those who suffer. When we order congregational life around the pain of the community and the pain of the world, we are following the example of the good Samaritan.

Of course, the parable of the good Samaritan goes far beyond functional and organized ways of reaching out. The eloquence of the parable calls upon every individual to bear witness to love in the face of suffering. Organizations and institutions are important, but they cannot be a replacement for deeds of mercy and kindness that grow out of love for others. Every time we practice love for a neighbor, we open up the possibility of giving birth to a civilization of love.

This moving parable teaches us to reach out to those who suffer—whether we do so as individuals or communities—because in so doing, we join the living Christ who is also compassionate toward those who are suffering. We can be a vessel through whom Christ can work if we follow the example of the good Samaritan.

As you thumb through the pages of this book, you will find many practical and constructive ways to reach out to those who are wearing the garments of suffering. As you do, you will become a modern-day good Samaritan; and as you are present to others, you will meet Christ there.

CHAPTER 2

The Ministry of Presence, Silence, and Sincerity

Physical presence, silence, and sincerity are of utmost importance as we reach out to those who suffer. The wise use of these three elements can communicate genuine care and concern. They also can demonstrate an openness to the pain of others.

Presence

When caring for those who suffer, we should not minimize the importance of physical presence. Nothing can replace being there with those who are in pain. Being present with those who suffer is, in fact, the greatest gift we can give because it communicates love made flesh.

At the age of two, our youngest daughter had surgery. The surgery was not classified as serious, but it was formidable for her mother and me. While she was in surgery, I looked across the hospital room and saw Travis, a member of a former congregation I had pastored, was standing in the frame of the door. He had driven 125 miles to see us. When our eyes met, he said, "I just came to be with you." The tone of his voice brought comfort to us although he did not talk much. He showed his love for us by simply being present. Travis did not have a high school education, but he was a very successful farmer who was deeply devoted to his faith. His way of showing concern was simply to be present with us, and he did that very well. His physical presence brought a comforting presence that embodied love for us. He did not communicate this love with words. He communicated it by just being there for us. That has been thirty-five years ago, but when I think about that day I still feel what I felt then. A phone call could not have communicated the same loving support.

Through the years as individuals and families in the churches I have served have experienced tragedy, loss, or illness, people have said to me, "I want to help, but I do not know what to say or what to do. If I wrote a note, I would not know what to say." Most of the time I have replied, "It is not what you say or do—just be present."

The Christian doctrine of the Incarnation is foundational to the ministry of presence. Just as God's love for us was incarnate in Jesus Christ, so also we strive to emulate and embody the love of God as we reach out to be with others. By being the hands and feet of Christ, the Word becomes flesh as we are present to those who suffer.

The ministry of presence is a way of "being" rather than a way of "doing" or "telling." As we prepare to be with those who suffer, we should not think about what to say or what to do. We should not anticipate how we might react if certain situations should develop. Instead, we should inwardly prepare ourselves to focus on the "now" with feeling and care. We should go with the earnest desire to emotionally participate in the space of those who suffer.

This ministry of presence is grounded in the belief that Christ goes before us. Shortly after I was ordained, a retired pastor said to me, "Joe, you are very fortunate to be able to carry Christ into the hospital room, into the funeral home, and into the homes of people." In time, I discovered that this retired pastor was sincere, but he was sincerely wrong. The spirit of Christ was already in the hospital room, the funeral home, and the homes of people. My task was simply to bear witness to the Christ who was already there. We all do this when we listen for the feelings behind the words, sit with others, offer a touch of the hand or a hug, and love them as Christ loves them.

That is the ministry of presence—to reflect the presence of Christ who always goes before us.

Silence

Reaching out to others does not always require the use of many words. Knowing when to be silent is also important. When caring for those who suffer, there often are times when silence, or quietness, is both appropriate and helpful. Before we explore this idea further, let us pause to consider how silence is also important *before* caring for those who suffer. Let me explain.

As caregivers, it is important that we practice the spiritual discipline of quietness in our daily lives. If we do not have our own quiet times, it will be difficult for us to practice quietness when the condition of the sufferer calls for it. It also will be difficult for us to hear and respond to the voice of God in the midst of our caregiving.

Because we must care for others in a hurried and noisy world that is filled with schedules, responsibilities, social requirements, and family needs, we can give the appearance of being present to others while neglecting the Christ that is within us. If we are not careful, the time we spend with those who suffer can keep us from taking time to prayerfully reflect on the motives that drive us, the feelings that block us, the desires that divert us, and the poisons that can infect our inner life. This kind of prayerful introspection can give us the inner strength that we need as we reach out to others. When we care for others in an attitude of prayer, we have the hope that our journey with those who suffer will open our hearts to God so that our hearts will be open to the pain of others. Through quietness, meditation, reflection, and contemplation we can seek the life that gives meaning to all of life. As we become aware of the presence of God through prayer and meditation, we can make space in our hearts to experience the God of Jesus in deeper and more profound ways. In so doing, we are better able to quietly connect with those who suffer.

If we neglect this silent part of our life, we will become like slaves to self-centeredness, which can block genuine care for others. Practicing quietness helps us to see the world as God sees, to think beyond our small agendas, to respond to the divine that is in all people, to weep for those who weep, and to cry with those who cry. Practicing quietness enables us to hear the voice of God in another, to see the face of God in the face of the other, and to be in touch with the pain that is in the lives of the one who is suffering.

Practicing silence in our own lives results in a quietness that flows from our interior life. This quietness generally is greatly appreciated by the sufferer—and often *needed*. In fact, we should always be prepared to be quiet if there is ever a need for silence. Whether or not you are comfortable with periods of undisturbed silence depends upon several factors. First, it depends upon the relationship you have with the sufferer. If there is trust, mutual interest, loyalty, family connections, and friendship, it is much easier to practice quiet tranquility. When the relationship is deep and long-standing, words are often better left unspoken. Words do not need to be used to build a relationship; the relationship precedes any vocabulary that we might choose to use. Periods of silence also can be helpful if we do not have a long-standing relationship with the sufferer. Empathy and careful listening have a way of communicating concern and care.

A friend of mine went to visit a neighbor whose son had committed suicide. My friend did not know the family very well, but he did not let that keep him from being present. When I went to see this family, they told me about the visit of my friend. They said, "He did not say much, but he was really with us, and he helped us by going to the door and by answering the phone." These neighbors will never remember what my friend said, but they will never forget his being there. My friend knew the value of empathetic silence. When ministering to suffering people, it is important to remember that we do not have to offer a cascade of words.

There is no prescription for when to be silent; it is something that is intuitive. There are, however, some general guidelines or "clues" that can help caregivers know when silence might be appropriate.

1. First, when ministering to those who have experienced loss, it is often appropriate for the caregiver to spend long periods of time in silence. In the face of great loss, words are often inadequate to express what we are feeling in our hearts. Moreover, when grief-stricken people ask "why," they are expressing grief more than asking some theological question. When this happens, it is better to use silence or to share a few words of empathy rather than to discuss what the Christian faith means by the doctrine of providence. It is also important to be silent when the grieving person tells and retells the story of what happened to cause the loss. As the story is being told, do not break in with opinions or advice. As the sufferer shares the story again and again, the loss will begin to lose its controlling power.

Likewise, a quiet presence can be helpful as persons are moving through the stages of grief: shock, depression, guilt, resentment, and the gradual rebirth of hope. Words will not talk people out of their feelings, but a listening ear can be extremely helpful.

2. Quietness also can be put to good use when visiting a person who is hospitalized. A patient who is tired, restless, or anxious might need to see the caregiver as a quiet and steadying influence. It is better not to ask questions such as, "What can I do?" or give advice such as, "Now try to get some sleep." Rather, it is often more helpful to stand quietly by—at ease, inwardly relaxed, and very empathetic.

We also should limit the use of words when there has been a loss of some physical faculty such as hearing, sight, speech, muscular strength, or mental processes. These losses can occur as a result of accident, illness, or the normal aging process. Reaching out to persons involved in the immediate crisis surrounding the onset of such losses does not require the use of many words. Preaching a "sermon" to such a person can do more harm than good. Rather, the caregiver can ask simple questions and have brief conversations about how the sufferer is coping. We reach out to such persons with the belief that God can work through us to bring about an adaptation to loss.

Obviously, I am not suggesting that one should never use words when ministering to those who suffer; but I do want us to know when silence is more important than the pounding of words. Knowing when words can be useful and when they can do harm enables us to minister effectively.

Sincerity

Finally, we come to sincerity. I cannot overemphasize the importance of sincerity when caring for those who suffer. Without sincerity, our presence and our silence mean nothing. The sufferer can tell if we are just "doing our duty" or if we are sincerely concerned. Insincerity is not helpful. People see right through it. When that happens, there is a failure of trust. And when trust is absent, there is a deep reluctance to share.

When I was the pastor of an inner city congregation, I served a parishioner who was an alcoholic and had an addiction to gambling. His sickness was widely known in the congregation. He was on my regular visitation list. He seemed to welcome my visits. I went to see him on a regular basis for over two years. His wife was never at home when I made my pastoral call because she was employed outside the home.

After three years in that congregation, I accepted an appointment to another congregation. On my final Sunday in that church, his wife bid me farewell by saying something such as this: "Thank you for all your visits to John. I want you to know that I really appreciate what you have tried to do for my husband. I need you to know what John said to me about your coming. He said, 'The preacher came around here all the time, but I am not sure that he really cared.' I do not want to hurt your feelings, but I thought that you needed to know how you came across."

John was correct in his assessment. My visits had been routine and pragmatic and without genuine feeling. I also was aware that the congregation knew I was being a pastor to John. I knew that the church members would look with favor on my work and would be pleased. In a word, I knew that I was helping my good standing in the congregation by visiting John.

If we are not sincere, there is the likelihood that we will not be empathetic. Empathy is the desire to identify with and experience what a sufferer is experiencing. We express empathy when we sincerely lay aside our prejudging and our frame of reference in order to enter the emotional world of another.

Empathy has a way of flowing from sincerity. If we are not sincere, empathy will not be self-evident. I cannot describe how to be sincere—we either are or we are not! However, we can be certain that those who suffer will be able to tell the difference. Sincerity cannot be faked. I was not sincere with John, and he knew it.

Empathy is vital if we are to be of help to those who suffer. If the sufferer truly feels that we care and that we are making every effort to understand, he or she is more apt to trust us by sharing deeper and deeper feelings.

We may not know what to say or what to do in every situation, but we can be sincere in our concern. Sincerely loving those who suffer can make up for not having the correct word or for some unintended action. When people feel loved in a nonjudgmental way, they are more apt to overlook our shortcomings and mistakes.

Reaching out to persons with presence, silence, and sincerity can be a great and good gift. It is a gift that God can use to bring consolation and hope.

CHAPTER 3

The Ministry of Words

When reaching out to those who suffer, it is crucial to remember the importance of words. Words have power. They can help or hurt, build up or tear down, heal or deepen a wound. Because words have such power, we need to take great care in how we use them. It is important to think about which words we will use *before* we use them. This is especially true with the spoken word.

The Spoken Word

In the previous chapter, I wrote about the importance of silence, but there comes a time to use the spoken word. We need to draw near with our speech while not being distant in our hearts. Reflective silence is the soil out of which helpful words can grow. Bombarding suffering persons with a barrage of words is not always helpful. Using a compassionate word in a timely fashion is far more useful. Here are some general guidelines about what to say and what not to say.

Choose Your Words Carefully

When reaching out to those who suffer, it is important to avoid rote sayings, such as "God never gives us more than we can bear" or "God needed her more than we did." Cathie, a friend of mine, lost her husband a few years ago. On one occasion I inquired, "Did well-meaning people say things to you that were not helpful?" She replied, "They certainly did. Many people said things like, 'God must have needed another angel in heaven.'" For several months, Cathie wanted her husband back, and she did not need to hear those words during the letting-go process.

Similarly, persons who are suffering from some form of unexpected adversity do not need to hear comments such as "This happened to teach us a lesson" or "Adversity builds character." I heard the latter said to a family whose house had burned to the ground, and I can assure you that it was not helpful!

Quoting certain passages of Scripture can be unhelpful, as well. Saying that suffering has come because our "parents have eaten sour grapes" (Ezekiel 18:2) or quoting verses such as "The descendants of the wicked will be cut off" (Psalm 37:28), "Prepare to meet your God" (Amos 4:12), and "I have destroyed my people; / they did not turn from their ways" (Jeremiah 15:7) can actually do more harm than good.

On the other hand, it is always helpful to quote texts that bring comfort, such as "[God] gives power to the faint, / and strengthens the powerless" (Isaiah 40:29), "In all these things we are more than conquerors through him who loved us" (Romans 8:37), and "Do not let your hearts be troubled, and do not let them be afraid" (John 14:27). I have found it helpful to memorize short verses of Scripture for easy reference. Those who suffer need to hear words from Scripture that witness to comfort and strength, as opposed to long exhortations.

As we think about what to say, we need to ask ourselves questions such as, *What would love have me to say? What word will bring comfort? What word will bring hope?* Likewise, we should consider making comments such as "I don't know what you are feeling, but I do want you to know that I care" and "My prayer is that you will feel the presence of Christ as you and your loved ones pass through this time." Since we are not all wired the same way, it is important for each of us to find our own voice and to speak with genuine concern.

When You Cannot Be Physically Present

Although the spoken word tends to be more effective when communicated in person, we should consider the value of expressing care and concern through a telephone call when we cannot be physically present. When I call someone who is suffering, I usually will say something such as, "Just calling to check on you to see how things are going." I then will let the person share whatever he or she wants me to know. After a brief conversation, I will say something such as, "I want you to know that I care, and I promise to hold you in the circle of my love and in my prayers." In my opinion, telephone conversations generally should be brief because we do not know what the other person is up against at that particular time.

Another good way to communicate care when we cannot be physically present is through the written word.

The Written Word

In addition to being physically present to those who suffer, we can be "present" to them through written communication. Expressing our love and concern in writing is an effective way to attend to those who suffer, particularly when we want to do something special.

Note Writing

A handwritten note can bring comfort and consolation when sent in a timely manner, such as at the time of suffering or just after the time of trial has passed. Waiting too long is not as helpful in providing comfort. When my mother died, for example, I received a note almost one year after her passing. It was a wonderful note, but it would have brought me more comfort if it had come much sooner.

Notes are a considerate way of offering care and concern. When I was a student at Vanderbilt Divinity School, Dr. Liston Mills taught courses in pastoral care. He was very careful to lecture about what constitutes a meaningful hospital visit. Once when he was hospitalized for several days, I visited him and asked what he needed from others while he was in the care of the hospital. Among other things he said, "I appreciated the notes because I could read them at my convenience, and I did not have to pay attention to every person who came through the door." That is one of the many values of notes. Sufferers can read them when they are ready.

J. Howard Olds, who is both a cancer patient and a pastor, writes this in his self-published booklet *Laughing and Crying Your Way Through Cancer*:

> Every day, for five months now, I have received cards and letters from friends near and far. I carve out a little time every day to open each one and to absorb its message. Some are humorous. Some are serious with verses of Scripture or poems of hope. A whole line of cards has now been

developed for cancer patients. One of my
favorite cards came from a golfing buddy.
With a lonely dog on the front it asked,
"How long until you can come out and
play?" Cards communicate support, love,
and concern. They are not intrusive. They
can be opened when a person feels like it,
which makes them most enjoyable.[1]

Persons and families who suffer have a
deep need to be in touch with others. Note
writing is one of the ways that this need can
be met. Notes can be held. Handwriting can
be seen. They can be kept by a bedside or displayed on a table or on the mantel as a con-
tinuing sign of care. It is my personal opinion
that greeting cards, voice mail, or e-mail mes-
sages do not trump the significance of a
handwritten note—though those methods of
communication have their time and place.
Genuine communication from the heart as
expressed in a handwritten note has a wonderful way of connecting to those who suffer.

As we think about note writing, we need
to be guided by some practical "guidelines."
I would like to suggest five:

1. Keep it brief and to the point. Notes do not need to be long dissertations or rambling sermons. When my mother died, I received enough cards and notes to fill a box. The vast majority of them simply said, "You are in our thoughts and prayers." It was nice to hear that, but there were times when I needed more. One of the most helpful notes came from a female parishioner I had served almost forty years ago. She is a gentle and hard-working farmer's wife who never went beyond high school. She never set foot on a college campus, but she is a very wise woman. Her note simply said, "Joe, you must believe that God will take care of you." That one sentence spoke volumes to me. It was just what I needed to hear. Often a few carefully chosen sentences can provide more comfort than a lengthy letter. Think about writing short notes that can be read quickly and that communicate bona fide concern for the one who is suffering.

2. Communicate support and care. Those who suffer do not need the latest magazine articles or news reports about the latest discoveries in medicine. Nor do they need theological or philosophical advice telling them how they should feel or act. I have discovered that not everyone responds to suffering in the same way, but almost everyone has good vibrations when they receive a note communicating support and care.

3. *Express love and hope.* Love and hope are two big words in Christian thought. When writing to the Hebrews, the apostle Paul said, "Let us hold fast to . . . our hope without wavering, for he who has promised is faithful" (Hebrews 10:23). Holding fast to hope is not like wishing. When we hold fast to hope, we affirm our belief that we will experience God in the midst of suffering. We also should clearly express our love for the sufferer. One of the ways to do this is to mention in the note some remembrance of a time when love was given and received. Sharing hope and love in these ways has the power to bring courage in the face of suffering. It can encourage people to keep on keeping on. There is no scientific formula for how this happens. It borders on being a mystery, but it is a reality.

4. *Share affirmation and appreciation.* If someone has been meaningful to you, tell the individual so in the note. People need to be appreciated for the contributions that they have made to our lives. Such affirmation might encourage the sufferer to persevere. When a pastor friend of mine was killed in an automobile accident, my brief note to his spouse said, "I am so very thankful that he was a servant of the servants of God." In my judgment, that was all that I needed to say at that time. I wrote a longer note a few days later.

5. *Write what you are feeling in your heart.* Writing a thoughtful note helps us to express what we are feeling in our heart. Sincerity is essential not only to the ministry of physical presence, but also to the ministry of the spoken word. When we take time to choose our words with care, prayerfully considering what needs to be said and how it might best be expressed, we communicate sincerity and genuine concern. Some "sample notes" that might be a helpful starting point as you contemplate what to say and how to say it are provided at the end of this chapter. In any event, it is important for the note to be in your own voice and not a copy of someone else.

As we write notes, let us not forget that the process of suffering will not be cheated. It will take as much time as it needs, and we cannot do anything to hasten its outcome. However, there is one thing that we can do: We can write a thoughtful note offering comfort and hope.

Practical Guidelines for Note Writing

1. Keep it brief and to the point.
2. Communicate support and care.
3. Express love and hope.
4. Share affirmation and appreciation.
5. Write what you are feeling in your heart.

E-mail and Other Electronic Communication

For those who are "computer friendly," e-mail and other forms of electronic communication are another way to express love, concern, affirmation, and support to those who are suffering. Although it is not recommended as the primary method of communication, e-mail is a quick and easy way to check in with someone and offer a brief word of encouragement between visits. Social networking websites such as Facebook and MySpace can be another effective tool when used appropriately and with sensitivity. For example, I have friends who are using Facebook as a way to communicate within their circle general details regarding struggles with health, hospitalizations, and various forms of brokenness. Given the community environment of such websites, this method of communication obviously is better suited for less personal or intimate exchanges. Although electronic communication will not work for everyone, it can be a good asset for those who are helped by it.

---

[1] *Laughing and Crying Your Way Through Cancer*, J. Howard Olds (self-published); p. 4.

Examples of
Notes of Encouragement

Grief

I hope you know how very thankful we are for you and all whom you love. As you learn to live with the loss of _____, I trust that you will be upheld by your family, your friends, and, most of all, your faith.

May you find comfort and strength in believing that love is stronger than death.

Death has power, but it does not have the capability to separate us from the love that you had for _____.

If I can be of any help, please do not hesitate to call.

In Christ,

Illness

_____ , I am very sorry that you have been sick. May the miracles of modern medicine and the presence of the Great Physician meet your every need at this time in your life. I am praying that God will grant you that which mortals do not know how to give, and that it will be given in great abundance.

If I can be of any help, please do not hesitate to ask.

In Christ,

Relocation

Having moved from one location to another, I know how traumatic this move can be for you and for those whom you love. It can also be difficult for those who remain in the former city/country.

We are hoping that your new city/ country will provide new opportunities for friendship, enrichment, and service to others.

If I can be of any help on this end, please do not hesitate to ask.

In Christ,

One Who Is Despondent

I understand that the troubles of your life are causing you to feel faint of heart and discouraged. It is my prayer and hope that you will soon have the courage and the power to go on your way and to be fully yourself in the days and years that lie ahead.

I want you to have all of the support that you need for the living of these days. I will be in touch to see if I can be of any help.

In Christ,

One Who Is Going Through a Divorce

I do not know what it is like to experience divorce, but I do know that "letting go" must be very difficult. It is my hope that you are being surrounded by some persons who have walked this same path. Also, I trust that you are feeling supported by family, friends, and your constant faith.

I sincerely want you to know that I stand ready to be of help. Please do not hesitate to call if you should need me.

In Christ,

Suicide

I was saddened to hear about the untimely death of _____. As time passes, may the treasured memories overcome your feeling of deep grief. May you soon come to the time when you remember and give thanks for those gifts that cannot be taken away.

As you emotionally walk through the processes of grief and healing, may you know that, in time, a new day will come.

I will be in touch to see if I can be of any help.

In Christ,

One Who Is Facing an Operation

I want you to know that I will be praying for a successful operation. I know that you will be in the good hands of doctors, nurses, and all who will attend to your needs. May God strengthen them for their task, and may they be fellow workers in the ministry of healing.

It is my hope that you will respond favorably and soon to the love and care that will be given.

I will be in touch with you in the very near future. In the meantime, if I can be of any help, please do not hesitate to call.

In Christ,

CHAPTER 4

The Ministry of Scripture and Prayer

God uses both Scripture and prayer to minister to those who are suffering. In fact, this is one of the primary ways that God reaches out to us. When we open ourselves to God by praying and reading the Bible, God is opened to us. As I have read Scripture and prayed with those who are suffering, I have experienced God unveiling God's identity and character in mystical but loving ways. Let us consider the usefulness of these two resources.

Scripture

"Holy Scripture is a stream of running water, where alike the elephant may swim, and the lamb walk without losing its feet." —*Pope Gregory the Great*

There are times when it can be helpful to read a passage of Scripture to those who are suffering. In so doing, we help the sufferer not to lose his or her feet.

Some Scriptures that are often useful when expressing care and concern for those who are suffering are provided in the Scripture Index (pp. 129–141). You also may want to select additional verses that speak to the specific needs or situations of the individuals you are caring for. In either case, it is of great importance to keep a few principles in mind as you make use of Scripture.

1. *Do not assume that the sufferer wants or desires Scripture to be read.* I have made it a practice to ask permission before reading. I say something such as, "Would it be helpful if I read a few verses of Scripture for you?" If there is hesitation in the answer, I simply say that we might do that at another time. If there is a desire for the reading, I proceed. I usually read Scripture near the end of my visit.

2. *Choose an appropriate text for the given situation.* For example, I would not suggest reading what the Bible says about divorce while people are in the midst of divorce proceedings. Nor would I suggest reading what Jesus said about anxiety for persons who are suffering from some extreme anxiety disorder. Whatever is read should reflect a deep sensitivity to the needs of the sufferer. I do believe that the Bible is the road or path to meeting the deeper needs of people, but we must be very careful to match the text selection with the particular needs of those who are caught in the web of suffering.

3. Recognize the power of Scripture and use it wisely. The biblical text has a certain dynamic power in and of itself. This has been described in many ways. For me, the biblical world has the power to disclose a new and different world. The biblical passage is not limited to what it is about on the surface—its topical references, stories, sayings, or poetry. Instead, the text can disclose a way of understanding that transcends the immediate situation. It has the strength to put one in touch with the transcendent and the holy. Both the reader of the text and the listener can be oriented toward the world that is disclosed by the thoughtful reading of the Bible.

This is more like a mystery than a fact, but I have found it to be true.

Dr. Liston Mills, professor of pastoral care at Vanderbilt Divinity School, was fond of saying that simply holding the *Prayer Book* or the Bible would bring comfort to some people. Although I have never been comfortable toting a large Bible around with me, I have been at ease carrying a small Testament or *Book of Worship* in my pocket. Having easy access to these resources can be helpful in certain situations.

The Bible has an almost mystical way of pointing beyond itself to the presence of a living God. It can be seen as a redemptive resource that has the power to strengthen those who suffer. Use it wisely, and use it carefully.

Principles for the Use of Scripture

1. Do not assume that the sufferer wants or desires Scripture to be read.
2. Choose an appropriate text for the given situation.
3. Recognize the power of Scripture and use it wisely.

Prayer

> "The pious ones of old used to wait a whole hour before praying, the better to concentrate their minds on God." —*The New Union Prayer Book*[1]

Prayer is our finite attempt to be open to the presence of the infinite. It opens our minds and hearts to the illumination of God. Through prayer we can experience the guidance of God to strengthen our hold on truth, goodness, righteousness, purity, and healing. When spoken from the heart, prayer has the power to bring us into the presence of God. Though it is not always easy and does not happen all at once or even every time, somehow praying from the heart and mind without reservation enables us to feel the holy in the midst of the commonplace.

Praying with those who suffer is a concrete expression of our caring. When we pray with an individual, he or she feels our concern at a deep and personal level. It also helps the person to compose his or her thoughts and feelings before God. It has a way of upholding the faith of those who suffer. Consider four ways that prayer can be helpful.

1. Prayer facilitates the healing of the body, mind, and spirit. It puts the sufferer in touch with a source that is beyond what mortals can do or understand. It also reminds the sufferer that there is a fountain of help that is deeper than the waters of modern medicine or psychology.

2. Prayer underscores the Christian belief in providence. Prayer reminds the Christian that God feels our pain even as Jesus experienced the agony of the cross. Although I do not believe that God wills pain, I do believe there is a redemptive potential in suffering. Prayer is a way of confirming and actualizing this resource.

3. Prayer assists us to be still, comforted, and secure in the sure knowledge of God's presence with us. Prayer can be a countermeasure to the stress of what might be a highly difficult situation. The psalmist put it like this: "Be still and know that I am God" (Psalm 46:10).

4. Prayer quickens the mind to be in a receiving mode. It is an expression of faith; and faith, at its best, is a way of receiving. Thus, when ending a prayer with someone who is suffering, we might say something such as, "May we be truly open to that for which we pray."

Four Ways That Prayer Can Be Helpful

1. Prayer facilitates the healing of the body, mind, and spirit.
2. Prayer underscores the Christian belief in providence.
3. Prayer assists us to be still, comforted, and secure in the sure knowledge of God's presence with us.
4. Prayer quickens the mind to be in a receiving mode.

Of course, it is vitally important for us to practice sensitivity when determining when to pray. Some caregivers rely on intuition when trying to understand when someone is receptive to prayer. I have found that one of the best ways is simply to ask. I usually say something such as, "Before I leave, would you like for me to offer a word of prayer for you?" In all of my years of being with those who suffer, there have only been a handful of times when persons refused my request. Obviously, prayer should never be forced on anyone; if the response is negative, we should accept it and pray for the person in our own intercessory prayer time.

Praying with those who suffer can be a very tender time, and often it causes emotions to surface. Do not be surprised if you see tears in the eyes of those who are suffering. Do not discourage the tears. Instead, give those suffering permission to freely express what they are feeling.

There are three ways of praying with those who suffer.

1. Praying extemporaneously. This is putting in your own words the needs and hopes of the one for whom you are praying. When I pray extemporaneously, I like to mentally follow the pattern of adoration, thanksgiving, intercession, and benediction. Keeping this simple formula in mind assists me in helping those who are the object of God's concern. You will want to find the prayer method that feels most comfortable for you. It is very important for us to be ourselves when we pray in this fashion. This is a time to be genuine, not artificial. If we seem manufactured, we will not bring the help that is needed.

2. Praying silently. There are times and places when it is appropriate to use silent prayer. You might say something such as, "If you would be comfortable, could we join hands and have a silent prayer? I would like to invite each of us gathered here to pray silently, and then I will conclude the prayer time." After the passing of some quiet time, conclude with a brief sentence prayer. I have found this approach to be helpful when I know that unbelievers, atheists, or agnostics are in the room. This gives them permission to pray, to think deeply, to connect emotionally, or simply to be silent in the face of suffering. Most of the time, great appreciation is offered when I give this permission.

3. Praying a printed or fixed prayer. The fixed prayer has value as a ready resource. Printed prayers can help us to put into words what people are feeling in their hearts. They can ensure that Christian ideals that have been learned over time will not perish from the community. They hold to the insights and truths that have come downstream to the community of faith. They also remind us that it is not we alone who pray. We are praying with others who have heard and said these very same words.

At the end of this chapter, you will find a variety of sample prayers that may be helpful to you as you are engaged in helping those who suffer.

The apostle Paul, in his first letter to the Thessalonians, said that we should "pray without ceasing" (5:17). I take this to mean that we should do everything prayerfully. Every form of reaching out to those who suffer should be done prayerfully. If we do not go about this ministry in a prayerful way, we will find ourselves relying on our own resources, and that will be inadequate to meet the need.

Ways of Praying With Those Who Suffer

1. Praying extemporaneously.
2. Praying silently.
3. Praying a printed or fixed prayer.

Sample Prayers

For the Sick

Kind and gracious Lord, please draw near to this your servant who now faces sickness. Give *him/her* the assurance that you are present and caring.

Look upon *him/her* with feelings of mercy and forgiveness. May *he/she* have a sure confidence in the comfort that you can bring. Defend *him/her* from danger of every sort, and grant unto *him/her* a sure feeling of perpetual peace and safety and the awareness of your constant healing presence; through Jesus Christ our Lord. Amen.

God of compassion, source of life and
    health;
strengthen and relieve your servant(s),
    Name(s),
and give your power of healing
  to those who minister to *their* needs,
that those for whom our prayers are
    offered

may find help in weakness
and have confidence in your loving care;
through him, who healed the sick
and is the physician of our souls,
even Jesus Christ our Lord. Amen.[2]

For a Sick Child

O God, we know that you have a child whose name is Jesus, so we have the awareness that you understand our feelings in this hour. Visit our child with your healing mercy and grant unto us all that we need to care for our *son/daughter*. Work through physicians and the miracles of modern medicine to deliver *him/her* from bodily sickness.

If *he/she* should be restored to health, may *he/she* live for your purposes, be an instrument of your glory, and be a vessel for doing good as long as *he/she* lives. May we as *parents/friends* know how to be helpful in this journey, and forgive us if we should make mistakes. Uphold our faith that we might trust you as never before.

Grant this for your mercy's sake in the name of your Son, our Lord Jesus

Christ, who lives and reigns in a world without end. Amen.

For a Person Facing Death

Dear God, we beg for you to listen to us. Draw near with your accustomed goodness to this your faithful servant who is grieving because of this illness. May *she/he* know your forgiving love in a deep and meaningful way. May this time of physical weakness be an opportunity for faith to be strengthened, love to be shared, and hope to be assured.

If it is your will to banish the illness and restore *her/him* to health, may *she/he* live the rest of *her/his* life to your glory and honor. If healing does not visit, may *she/he* welcome your eternal presence, and after this pain is ended, may *she/he* dwell with you in everlasting peace; through Jesus Christ our Lord. Amen.

For Those Who Mourn

Gracious God,
as your Son wept with Mary and Martha

at the tomb of Lazarus,
look with compassion on those who grieve,
[especially *Name(s)*].
Grant them the assurance of your presence now
and faith in your eternal goodness,
that in them may be fulfilled the promise
that those who mourn shall be comforted;
through Jesus Christ our Lord. Amen.[3]

Ministry With Persons Suffering From Addiction or Substance Abuse

God of mercy,
we bless you in the name of your
Son, Jesus Christ,
who ministered to all who came to
him.
Give your strength to *Name*, your servant,
[bound by the chains of addiction].
Enfold *him/her* in your love
and restore *him/her* to the freedom of
your children.
Look with compassion on all those who
have lost their health and freedom.
Restore to them the assurance of your
unfailing mercy.

Strengthen them in the work of recovery,
[and help them to resist all temptation].
To those who care for them,
grant patient understanding and a
love that perseveres.
We ask this through Christ our Lord.
Amen.[4]

Ministry With Persons With AIDS

Most merciful God, you hold each of us
dear to your heart.
Hold *Name(s)* in your loving arms
and tenderly draw *them* into your love,
together with all who are living with
AIDS and HIV infection.
Assure them that they are not alone,
and give them courage and faith for
all that is to come.
Strengthen those who care for them and
treat them,
and guide those who do research.
Forgive those who have judged harshly,
and enlighten those who live in prejudice or fear.
Nourish those who have lost sight of you,
and heal the spirits of those who are
broken.

We pray this in the name of Jesus, who
     suffered and died,
   and then rose from the dead to lead
   us into new life,
   now and forever. Amen.[5]

Ministry With Persons With Life-Threatening Illness

Lord Jesus Christ,
   we come to you sharing the suffering
   that you endured.
Grant us patience during this time,
   that as we and *Name* live with pain,
   disappointment, and frustration,
   we may realize that suffering is a part
   of life,
   a part of life that you know inti-
   mately.
Touch *Name* in *his/her* time of trial,
   hold *him/her* tenderly in your loving
   arms,
   and let *him/her* know you care.
Renew us in our spirits,
   even when our bodies are not being
   renewed,
   that we might be ever prepared to
   dwell in your eternal home,

through our faith in you, Lord Jesus,
  who died and are alive for evermore.
Amen.[6]

Ministry With Persons Going Through Divorce

God of infinite love and understanding,
pour out your healing Spirit upon *Name*,
  as *he/she* reflects upon the failure of
  his/her marriage
    and makes a new beginning.
Where there is hurt or bitterness,
  grant healing of memories
    and the ability to put behind the
    things that are past.
Where feelings of despair or worthless-
    ness flood in,
  nurture the spirit of hope and confidence
    that by your grace tomorrow can be
    better than yesterday.
Where *he/she* looks within and discov-
    ers faults
  that have contributed to the destruction of the marriage
    and have hurt other people,
  grant forgiveness for what is past

and growth in all that makes for new
life.
[Heal *children's names*, and help us minister your healing to *them*].
We pray for [other] family and friends,
for the healing of their hurts and the
acceptance of new realities.
All this we ask in the name of the One
who sets us free from slavery to the
past and makes all things new,
even Jesus Christ our Savior. Amen.[7]

For Loss After Pregnancy

Ever-loving and caring God,
we come before you humbled by the
mysteries of life and death.
Help us to accept what we cannot understand,
to have faith where reason fails,
to have courage in the midst of disappointment.
Comfort *mother's Name*, who has lost a
part of herself,
and *Names of father and/or other family
members*.
Help *them (her)* to see the hope of life
beyond grief.

Through Jesus we know that you love
all your children
and are with us always.
Let us feel that presence now as we seek
to live in faith,
through Jesus Christ our Lord. Amen.[8]

For Those Who Suffer

"Let Me See Light"

Where are you, Lord? My heart is
aching. Let me see the light of your
love. Let me see a glimmer of hope.
I am lost in a dark tunnel of suffering,
and desperately searching to find my
way out.
May I feel your arms reach out to
embrace me and hold me close.
May I hear your words spoken to
comfort, guide, and give me peace.
May I experience your touch
through acts of love and caring to
cover me with compassion.
Let me see the cross and know that absolutely nothing can ever separate me
from your love. Amen.

—*Sue Downing*

For Those Who Care for the Suffering

"Let Your Light Shine Through Me"

Show me the way, Lord. My heart is aching for those who suffer.

Let the light of your love shine through me.

Open my eyes that I might see the real needs in a hurting world.

Open my ears that I might hear the cries for help.

Open my arms that I might reach out and draw your children near to me.

Open my hands so that I can freely give the gifts that I alone have to offer.

Open my heart so that the light of your love can be a beacon of hope to the suffering. Amen.

—*Sue Downing*

---

[1] *Gates of Prayer: The New Union Prayer Book* (CCAR Press, 1975); p. 3.

[2] #457 from *The United Methodist Hymnal* © 1989 by The United Methodist Publishing House. Used by permission.

[3] #461 from *The United Methodist Hymnal* © 1989 by The United Methodist Publishing House. Used by permission.

CHAPTER 5

Seven Simple Do's and Don'ts

I have alluded to a number of "do's" and "don'ts" in previous chapters, but I have chosen seven significant ones to highlight here so that you may have quick-and-easy access to specific, practical things to keep in mind when reaching out to those who are traveling the winding road of suffering. This chapter is intended to serve as a quick reference guide that you may flip back to again and again.

1. Be a good listener.

Advice from the ancient Book of Ecclesiastes is still worth heeding. The writer says, "Let your words be few" (5:2). A New Testament writer echoes the words of Ecclesiastes by saying, "Let every person be quick to listen, slow to speak" (James 1:19). In the early church, the work of deacons with the sick and needy implies a generalized listening ability. Today, listening has a responsible and legitimate place in the shepherding ministry of the church.

When being present with those who suffer, work on practicing active listening rather than passive listening. In active listening, we try to listen beyond signs, words, and sounds to really hear what is going on in the depths of a person's soul. This is not a simple act. It is a difficult art, and it is very hard work. Most of us are conditioned to talk rather than listen. When we truly listen, we engage the sufferer in a deeper caring relationship.

From the vantage point of the sufferer, there is therapeutic value in feeling that someone cares enough to listen carefully and deeply. Such listening also gives birth to trust, which is one of the foundations of a caring relationship.

2. Do not say, "I know how you feel."

The truth is that we do not know how another person feels. If we have never experienced divorce or cancer or being robbed or whatever the person's experience may be, we do not know how that person feels. Saying "I know how you feel" may seem to be a way of saying "I care," but it is not a good way to sympathize with the feelings of another. I have a friend whose wife died of cancer, and he said that he grew weary of hearing people say, "I know how you feel." He commented that others had no way of knowing how much he loved his wife, and then he made a rather profound statement: "I have discovered that the more you love someone, the more you will grieve." Even if my wife had died of cancer, I could not have known how he felt because every context is different.

It is better to say, "Tell me how you are feeling," rather than "I know how you feel." It is more desirable to listen deeply than to bombard the person with opinions and words.

3. Do not be a busybody.

Prying around in people's feelings is not the task of the caregiver. I received an e-mail from a mother who was sharing that her daughter-in-law had just left her son and their two children. She left home for a few days and then came back to gather up her things. As I read the e-mail, I could feel the brokenness in the mother and in the entire family. I wanted to know more: *What had caused her to leave? What had gone wrong in the marriage? Was there some mental illness? How were the children responding?* However, it was clear from the woman's e-mail that she had told the receivers of her correspondence all she wanted them to know. I wrote her back, indicating my concern for all members of the family and offering to be of help if she needed me. I also made a commitment to be prayerful. If this mother wanted me to know more, she would share it when the time was right. I needed to honor her feelings by not poking around in the lives of her family. To do so would have violated her trust in me.

Rather than pry into the circumstances, it is better simply to receive whatever the sufferer is willing to give. If we communicate genuine care, the time will come when more will be shared.

4. Do not overstay your visit.

Long visits do not necessarily mean helpful visits. Suffering does not always leave an individual with enough energy for long visits or lighthearted conversation. It is important to stay focused on the sufferer and the family of the one who is suffering. In so doing, we can work toward a meaningful visit. Unless the one who is suffering is sharing from his or her heart, it is better to stay briefly. Only if the sufferer is sharing something important is it advisable to stay longer.

I remember making a house visit to a very fine lady who was being cared for by Alive Hospice. I had planned to make a brief but meaningful visit. However, when I had been with her for only a few minutes, she started talking about funeral requests. I stayed until she had told me all that she wanted me to hear. The visit was much longer than usual, but it was important that I remain as long as I was needed. "Stay only as long as you are needed" is a good rule of thumb.

5. Avoid using rote sayings.

You do not need a bag full of sayings. As I've mentioned previously, saying something such as "God never gives us more than we can bear" or "This happened to teach us a lesson" is generally not helpful. It is better to choose words that are filled with hope and compassion, and it is more advantageous if these words grow out of careful listening rather than rote sayings.

Rather than offering rote sayings, find your own voice and speak comforting and encouraging words with genuine concern. If you find yourself at a loss for words, it is far better to offer an embrace or a simple expression of love and care than to fill the silence with a rote saying.

6. Offer practical help.

Suffering individuals and families often need practical help with daily or routine tasks such as cutting the grass, going to the grocery, running errands, keeping the children, sitting with elderly parents, or cleaning the house. Many people are often reluctant to request this kind of help, which is why it is important for us to offer it. Such offers generally are received as expressions of love and concern. If people know that we are willing to help in practical ways, they are more likely to make requests.

People who are grieving or going through a life-threatening illness will find it helpful if we invite them to make a list of things that others might do for them. If these offers are made in a genuine way, sufferers are more inclined to receive volunteer efforts to be of service.

If the sufferer should refuse the help that is offered, an appropriate response would be something such as, "I understand. But if you change your mind or if the circumstances change, I hope you will not hesitate to ask. It will help others to help you." If you feel that assistance is truly needed, write a note making a second offer to be of help with the everyday tasks of life.

7. Listen to the stories.

I have discovered that suffering people find some solace in telling stories about their lives. When those who suffer share their stories with us, they are inviting us to come into their life experiences. Storytelling has two important and related effects. First, it breaks down barriers and removes the masks that prevent individuals from sharing their pain. It frees them from experiencing the added hurt that comes from the isolating effect of suffering. Simply put, storytelling helps people to share their pain. Second, when we are invited into an individual's story, a depth of understanding results that would not be possible otherwise. Sharing a story creates a richness that cannot be achieved by simply stating facts.

If families or individuals want to tell their stories, it is important to listen not only with our ears but also with our hearts. When we listen with our ears, we are trying to hear the feelings behind the words. When we listen with our hearts, we are letting compassion tune into what is being said. Though the one who is suffering needs both kinds of listening, listening with the heart tends to require more patience because suffering people often retell the same stories with the same details. As caregivers, we must be careful not to say, "You've told me that story before. I know what you are saying." The telling and retelling of a story is a way that many people adapt to loss and suffering.

Recently, I went to see a widow whose husband had died six months earlier. She told me the same narrative that she had told me on the occasions of my previous visits. When she realized that she was repeating herself, she said, "The death of my husband has totally disrupted my life, and the rehearsing of his death has helped me to adapt to life without him." She was beginning to see the present as having meaning and the future as having hope. I do not know how it works, but I do know that trodding the familiar ground over and over again helps those who suffer to reorder life.

As we listen to the stories of others, we offer a place of safety and comfort, even as they explore their questions and look for sacred acts of healing. Those who suffer have a much better chance of finding the strength to "live" again if we listen to their stories and lovingly walk beside them.

Seven Simple Do's and Don'ts

1. Be a good listener.
2. Do not say, "I know how you feel."
3. Do not be a busybody.
4. Do not overstay your visit.
5. Avoid using rote sayings.
6. Offer practical help.
7. Listen to the stories.

PART 2

Understanding the Responses of Those Who Suffer

The experience of suffering is not transferable. Each individual's journey is unique, and there are as many responses to suffering as there are causes of suffering. Making sense of suffering is not limited to one absolute view.

CHAPTER 6

Common Responses to Suffering

I have spent most of my life observing the community of suffering from a front-row seat, one close enough to see the breaking of hearts, to share the pain of others, and to feel the tears running down my own cheeks. Sitting in this front-row seat has introduced me to many different causes of suffering—hurtful or broken relationships, illness, accidents, death, suicide, moral failure, greed, loneliness, rejection, poverty, prejudice, hate, war. The list could go on and on. We simply cannot escape suffering in this world. We do not have to go looking for it. It faces us at every turn. No one will be left untouched.

Suffering has a way of creating another "world" or realm of experience. Suffering drags people away from their everyday homeland and causes them to live in a kind of dispersion. This new world has its own sights, sounds, vocabulary, techniques, therapies, and medications.

Yet those who suffer do not live alone in this new world. They are in strong solidarity with others who suffer. I have noticed that a powerful bond exists between both strangers and friends who are walking the road of suffering. When they meet on this road, there is an instant connection.

My wife and I experienced this lesson firsthand a few years ago when she had a heart attack. She was brought into solidarity with others who had the same experience. There was a powerful kinship between my wife and others who had heart problems and had experienced intensive care, rehabilitation, special diets, exercise programs, and the care and understanding of others. This experience taught us anew that the world of suffering creates its own sense of community. Any visit to a hospital waiting room will put one in touch with the reality of shared suffering, which can be a source of both comfort and hope.

Despite this community and camaraderie of those who walk the road of suffering, the experience of suffering is not transferable. Each individual's journey is unique, and there are as many responses to suffering as there are causes of suffering. My life as a pastor has taught me that people understand and respond to suffering in various ways. Making sense of suffering is not limited to one absolute view. Understanding some of the common understandings and responses people have regarding suffering can help us to meet people where they are.

In this chapter I share a few of the common responses to suffering, although this list is not exhaustive. As caregivers, we should not try to talk someone out of his or her response, because each response is real to the one who is suffering. We are not called to lecture people out of their understandings. Our task is to minister to people at whatever point we find them, regardless of their theology. We have the privilege of reaching out with compassion, trusting God to alter any wrong understandings. With some individuals, these responses will overlap; an individual might express more than one at a time. In any case, if we have clues about how persons are responding, we will be better prepared to respond to them.

1. "Suffering is the result of sin."

Some religious people have tried to erase the connection between sin and suffering. These people of faith dismiss the idea of sin in a causative sense. They tend to look at suffering in a more scientific way—medically, physiologically, psychologically, or sociologically. However, if we think of sin as any thought, word, or deed that separates us from ourselves, our neighbors, or God, then we must say that separation in whatever form is the cause of much of the world's suffering.

The Old Testament writers clearly saw suffering as a penalty for sin, and great suffering as the punishment for great wickedness. Second Kings portrays a people who see their land destroyed and who go into captivity because of their sins. The First Psalm talks about how the way of the wicked shall perish. Job's friends say that Job is guilty because of his sin. Furthermore, the ultimate penalty for sin is death (Genesis 2:17).

In the New Testament, the Hebrew notion that suffering is the result of sin is uttered by Jesus when he says to the man who had been healed, "See, you have been made well! Do not sin any more, so that nothing worse happens to you" (John 5:14). Yet the New Testament offers a remedy for sin. This is why Christ came: "he will save his people from their sins" (Matthew 1:21), he is "the lamb of God who takes away the sin of the world" (John 1:29), he came "to call not the righteous but sinners" (Matthew 9:13), "the Son of Man came to seek out and to save the lost" (Luke 19:10). Like John the Baptist, Jesus came preaching repentance and forgiveness (Matthew 9:2; 18:3).

I have heard people say with strong conviction that suffering is a just reward for evil or sinful living. For example, on the days that followed Hurricane Katrina, more than one preacher said the storm was a punishment for the sinfulness of New Orleans. Those who spoke this way had the conviction that God destroyed parts of New Orleans as a way of sending a message to the rest of America. That message was clear and simple: Clean up your act or the same things might happen to you and those whom you love.

During the late sixties, I served as a volunteer chaplain to a large youth detention center. My trips to the facility produced many interesting conversations with the guards and staff. Many of these custodians had worked in that environment for so long that they had become hardened to the pain and suffering that filled every corner of every room. On more than one occasion, a guard would say to me, "These kids are getting what they deserve." To them, suffering in jail was a just reward for wayward living.

I once was pastor to a man who was unfaithful to his wife. The affair lasted for months. He was planning to divorce his wife when his son was diagnosed with brain cancer. With tears pouring down his cheeks, he told me that he was being punished for the relationship. I tried to help him view things differently, but he could not see it any other way. I took the wrong approach in trying to change his mind, because this was the only way that he could make sense out of the bind that he was in. For him, there was a cause and effect at work. It was more important for me to be a means of grace for him as I tried to act in a redemptive way. So I went to see the man, wrote him notes, and made phone calls. Finally, the time came when I could say, "I forgive you, and so does your wife." After a long pause, he said, "If you can forgive me, I guess Christ does also."

When ministering to those who are suffering as a result of sin, we need to convey the spirit of reconciliation and forgiveness. We must never forget that the church is a redemptive community, and as such we need to offer words and deeds of mercy and kindness to those who are separated and broken because of sin. As those who reach out to people who are suffering, it is important for us to accept people where they are in a nonjudgmental way. If we will embody the love of Christ and practice a forgiving spirit toward those who believe their circumstances are the result of sin, we can help them to accept the sure belief that they are loved in spite of their sin and subsequently provide a step toward healing.

2. "Suffering is a means of discipline or instruction."

Another common response to suffering is to say that it is a way of imposing discipline on us. It teaches us a lesson like a parent disciplining a child in order to teach a greater truth.

A number of years ago, the congregation I was serving started a career transition support group. The purpose of this gathering was to provide a supportive community for persons who had lost their jobs or who were caught in some vocational transition. Some were without work, while others were employed but wanted to look for other opportunities. This support group dealt with such issues as networking, preparing resumes, building relationships, discovering one's strengths, and drawing on spiritual resources.

During one of the meetings, a man stood up and said, "Let us not forget that our job loss is God's way of teaching us something that we need to learn." This response to suffering stems from the belief that God disciplines us through suffering as a way of teaching greater moral, ethical, and spiritual lessons. Many people hold to his understanding.

My childhood pastor would often refer to this idea as "soul building." People who hold this view of suffering see a positive side. They see suffering as a way to build human character. The prophet Isaiah wrote about the "bread of adversity" opening the eyes and ears so that the proper path could be taken (Isaiah 30:20-21).

In reaching out to persons who hold this position, it is important to affirm that we can learn valuable lessons as a result of suffering. We can reach out with warmth and accept-ance without taking on a directing posture. Shifting the focus to what we can learn from suffering is more important than a theologi-cal discussion about God's intentions to dis-cipline us by causing us to suffer. It is possible to affirm "learning" without agree-ing or disagreeing with the premise.

3. "Suffering is intended to help us see what is truly important."

A third response to suffering is that all suf-fering is intended to be revelational. In other words, it helps us to see what truly counts in life. It forces us to revalue our values.

For example, I know a woman who was diagnosed with ovarian cancer a number of years ago. Prior to this diagnosis, she worked as the assistant manager to the regional manager for a large retail company. She had worked in that capacity long enough to be highly valued and fully vested. Everyone acknowledged that her competence was far above average. She faced her cancer with a high level of resolve, and after many months of treatment, she went into remission.

It was during that period of her life that she thought deeply and prayerfully about her vocation. After she went into remission, I invited her to use her many gifts as an administrative assistant on our church staff. She readily accepted my invitation because she had come to believe that God was calling her to a life of service in the church. She would say that her war with cancer was revelational. It opened her up to new possibilities for her life. Although my friend would not say that God sent cancer as a way of causing her to travel another vocational path, some would say that cancer was indeed God's way of bringing her to consider a new vocation.

I do not believe that God initiates suffering as a way of getting us to find a new path, but I do believe that in the midst of suffering the Holy Spirit has a way of nudging us to revalue our values and perhaps to shift our priorities. As caregivers, we should find ways to assist persons who are being made open to new possibilities for living. Suffering, paradoxically, can lead to new life. Much depends upon how a person handles suffering, as well as the care that is given.

4. "Suffering is illusory."

Another response to suffering says that all suffering is illusory. I have not witnessed this understanding often, but I have heard it enough to know that some people do in fact possess this point of view. Such people believe that physical suffering has no biological cause and is rooted in a distorted psychological condition. "You are not really sick; you just think you are" is the way this view has been expressed to me. One church member told me that if people would see life as it really is, much suffering would go away. According to this logic, if we will adjust to reality, handle our anxieties, and face life, then suffering will not come knocking at our doors.

The Bible does not say that suffering is illusory. The Bible portrays people who face and live with real suffering. It tells about people who suffer in many ways and who struggle to understand the meaning of suffering. The Gospels portray a world that has a firsthand experience with suffering. The sick and suffering crowd the gospel drama. In the midst of this world of suffering, the Gospels portray Jesus as being in solidarity with those who are in pain. He touches the sick, and in his passion he joins the ranks of those who suffer.

No, suffering is not fake. It was real for Jesus. In the Gospels of Matthew and Mark, Jesus cries out, "My God, my God, why have you forsaken me?" (Matthew 27:46; Mark 15:34). His suffering was not playacting. As caregivers, we must never forget that it was from the suffering of Jesus that God brought forth new life, and that it is from all suffering that God can bring transformation and new life. It is out of this conviction that we reach out to those who suffer.

5. "Suffering can be prevented or cured by a strong faith."

Some people say that much suffering is caused or prolonged by a lack of faith. They often believe that medications are not needed because strong faith can bring about a desired cure. This line of thinking places strong emphasis on supernatural intervention that results in miracles.

A friend of mine started what he called a "healing ministry." He purchased and moved into an old commercial building for the purpose of this ministry. He used media, pamphlets, and word of mouth to attract those who were sick in mind, body, and soul. He believed that he had the power to heal, which he saw as a gift from God. He believed that this gift was unique to some people but not shared by many. The foundation for his theology was the idea that physical, mental, and emotional suffering is caused by a lack of faith. He did not trust medical interventions such as chemical agents, x-rays, or operations. He was convinced that a lack of faith causes suffering and a strong faith results in a cure.

He would talk with me about an energy that would flow through his body toward the person in need of healing. He told me about laying his hands on a sick child and feeling his hands begin to vibrate with an intense heat. This, as he understood it, was healing power flowing through his body to hers. He claimed that she was healed because of his gift and her faith.

For my friend and for many others who share this view, a strong faith both prevents and cures suffering.

Though I do not subscribe to the "healing ministry" as expressed by my friend, I do understand that some measure of faith was normally evoked by Jesus as a condition of healing (Matthew 9:29; Luke 17:19; 18:42). Also, certain healings took place without any specific mention of faith being present (Matthew 9:1-8; 12:9-13; Luke 13:11-13; 14:4; 22:51). Since Jesus experienced pain and suffering on the cross, and since he was concerned about the frail, feeble, and broken of body and soul, it is appropriate to pray for healing as well as spiritual restoration. As you read the prayers in Chapter 4, you see that I do believe that faith has a place in the healing process.

As caregivers, we need to remember that it is God who works through the miracles of modern medicine and the presence of others to bring about either physical or spiritual healing.

6. "Suffering is proof that God is uncaring, inactive, incompetent, or nonexistent."

Sometimes individuals respond to suffering by concluding that God is uncaring or uninvolved, is unable to do anything, or does not exist. I knew a man who maintained that the widespread suffering in the world proved to him that God does not exist. "If there is a God," he said, "this God must be inactive or uncaring." He went on to say something along these lines: "People of faith are sincere, but they are mistaken about a God who would intervene in the affairs of people who are suffering." According to his logic, neither faith nor science can prove or disprove the existence of God; so we should not let either position shed light on an adequate response to suffering.

This man is a very fine person who would be quick to say that we are obligated as members of the human family to respond with compassionate care to those who are trapped in the web of suffering. He is deeply committed to the ethic of love and justice. He firmly believes that the purpose of his life is to increase love in the world. Yet he cannot have faith in a God who permits suffering of any sort.

In one of our conversations, I asked him if he believed in love. He answered with a strong "yes" to that question. So I pushed him by saying, "How can you believe in love? You cannot touch it, smell it, hear it, or understand how it works. How, then, can you believe it to be true?" He answered, "I believe in love because I can see the results of love." I responded, "If I argued that God is love, would that make a difference?" "No," he said, "because a loving God would not permit suffering in the world."

The problem of suffering has proven to be a stumbling block for many who are ethical and loving, while it has led others to believe in a God who is embracing, rescuing, benevolent, and meaning-giving. Caregivers who minister to persons who are agnostic or atheist need to be nonjudgmental while loving the individual after the example of Christ Jesus. If we practice the kind of love that points beyond itself to the God who is love, perhaps such persons will be moved toward faith.

7. "Suffering is a mystery."

Finally, some people respond to suffering by acknowledging that it is a mystery. This is very difficult for some, because we live in a world that places more emphasis on mastery than on mystery. Those who see life this way would say that mystery is inherent in all deep human experiences, and that it points beyond itself to that which is numinous or ultimately spiritual.

We can try to understand suffering and still not know all there is to know. I would contend that suffering is a mystery because God is a mystery. God is both revealed to us and hidden from human sight at the same time. Humans do not have a direct line to all there is to understand about God. Rational examination will not open the doors of our minds so that we can fully comprehend the infinite. The Hebrew Bible has much to say about the activity of God, but it does not claim to make a full acknowledgment. In Deuteronomy 29:29, Moses says, "The secret things belong to the LORD our God, but the revealed things belong to us and to our children forever, to observe all the words of this law." Likewise, Jesus spoke about "the secret of the kingdom of God" (Mark 4:11), and the apostle Paul spoke about the apostles being "stewards of God's mysteries" (1 Corinthians 4:1).

I join those who believe that mystery can be experienced in the wonders of nature, artistic beauty, scientific discovery, and human compassion. It also can be experienced as we walk the trodden road of suffering. When mystery surfaces in unexpected and unplanned ways, it can point in convincing ways to that which is transcendent and holy. Mystery has a way of pointing beyond itself to the greater mystery of life.

We need to affirm those who see suffering as a mystery. Do not try to rationalize them out of this understanding. If we can accept God as one who acts in mysterious ways, surely we can attest to the mystery of suffering. As caregivers, we need to keep alive the mystery so that care receivers can have the opportunity to experience the mystery of God's perspective with those who suffer.

Some Common Responses to Suffering

1. "Suffering is the result of sin."
2. "Suffering is a means of discipline or instruction."
3. "Suffering is intended to help us see what is truly important."
4. "Suffering is illusory."
5. "Suffering can be prevented or cured by a strong faith."
6. "Suffering is proof that God is uncaring, inactive, incompetent, or nonexistent."
7. "Suffering is a mystery."

Your Response to Suffering

As I mentioned at the beginning of this chapter, this is not an exhaustive list of responses to suffering; these are merely the ones I have encountered most often in my years of ministry. It will be helpful to you to list other responses to suffering that you have observed or experienced. Take a moment to do that now.

Other responses to suffering:

_____

_____

_____

_____

_____

_____

Of all the responses to suffering discussed in this chapter, including those you have just listed, *what is your personal response to suffering?* As a caregiver, it is important for you to understand how you respond to suffering. It is not easy to come to a self-understanding regarding your own response to suffering, but it is beneficial because you need a vantage point as you relate to those who suffer. Ludwig Feuerbach wrote, "What is finite to the understanding is nothing to the heart."[1] If we look at suffering with our hearts and try to understand as much as we can with our finite minds, we will be more able to connect in loving ways with those who suffer.

At the same time, it is necessary to be patient and understanding with those who might hold a different view than you do. Your role as caregiver is not to convert people to your point of view; nor are you obligated to give pat answers to complicated and difficult questions. Rather, it is your task to identify with the pain, to be empathetic, to hear the words behind the feelings, and to communicate deep care and genuine concern.

---

[1] *The Essence of Christianity* (Prometheus Books, 1989); p. 6.

CHAPTER 7

God and Human Freedom

If we are to understand the responses of those who suffer and thus be better equipped to help them, we need to give thought to the subject of God and human freedom. I say this because much of the world's suffering grows out of a misuse of freedom. In this chapter, we will explore God's gift of freedom—not only to human beings, but also to the universe—and how this relates to human suffering. We also will consider some practical ways that we can use our gift of freedom to respond to those who suffer in compassionate and caring ways.

Human Freedom Gives Us Choice

The Creation stories in the Bible speak about a God who freely created humans and who gave us the freedom, or free will, to make choices and determine how we are to live. We are free to do good or evil, to do that which is right or that which is wrong. We can choose to practice love or to join the powers of evil. We are free to cooperate with God's intentions for humankind, and we are fully capable of thwarting God's desire that we live responsible and loving lives.

The Hebrew Bible is filled with examples of how the Israelites chose not to obey God and not to keep the covenant. They were free to choose obedience, yet often they chose disobedience. Likewise, the New Testament tells about how the first disciples chose not to follow Jesus as he moved toward Jerusalem. The Book of Acts and the letters of Paul tell many stories about how the early church struggled with decisions about whether to obey or disobey the teachings of Jesus. Jesus himself demonstrated freedom by choosing to go to the cross as an act of sacrificial love. He was willing to suffer his own death as a sign of his devotion to God.

For a number of years I met with a large delegation of youth each year at annual conference (a regional gathering of United Methodists) for a time called "Conversations

With the Bishop." We would talk about various topics and try to apply the teachings of Jesus to the life issues that the young people were facing. On one of those evenings, we were having some rather interesting conversation around the topic of what God can and cannot do. Some of the youth were very vocal and deeply committed to the belief that God could be blamed or given credit for everything that happens. One of the youth said, "God can drive a nail in that wall if God wants to." Another youth jumped to her feet and said, "Sure, God could do that, but God would not do so because God wants us to have the freedom to drive the nail in the wall."

Without fully understanding what she was saying, that young lady was articulating a theological position that God chooses to limit God's power in order to grant freedom to humankind. God has given us the freedom to make choices.

Human Freedom Has Limits

Although we are free to make choices, this freedom has its limitations because not every decision is totally up to us. In a word, we have limited, not unlimited, freedom.

For example, we have limited choices in the living of our lives. Many of my choices are limited because I was born in a white, male body. I have the genes of my parents, I was educated in public schools in the South, and I was taught to view the world in a certain way. I can change some things in my life, but I cannot change everything. Similarly, when my wife had a heart attack a few years ago, she discovered that she could change her eating habits, her exercise, and her medications, but she could not change her genes.

In all of our lives, there is that which we can control and that which we cannot control; that which we can change and that which we cannot change. Thus, our freedom is a limited freedom.

We Can Misuse Our Freedom

One of the things in life that we absolutely cannot change is the fact that we are loved by God. God loves us, and we cannot do anything about that. A sign of God's love for us is that life comes to us as a sheer gift. Every day is a rare and special gift. Every raindrop that falls and every flower that buds is a gift. Every opportunity to have a significant relationship is a gift.

Not all people believe that. Some people believe that life is an entitlement rather than a wonderful gift. Yet the truth is that we do nothing to earn each new day. It is an unmerited gift. Those who see life as an entitlement find many reasons to use human freedom to exploit life for gain or to take advantage of others. Those who see life as a gift, on the other hand, have a tendency to reverence life and to enhance it for others. They also have a wonderful way of looking for the holy in the everyday things of life.

The God who loves us and grants life to us as a gift has a strong and abiding desire that we should love one another. God longs for us to use the freedom that we have to love one another and to care deeply for creation. I believe that God has a dream that we will use what we do control to do what is just and loving toward others. Much suffering comes to the human family, however, when we misuse our freedom by not doing what love and justice require. This misuse of freedom results in sin.

As I've mentioned previously, sin is any thought, word, or deed that brings separation—separation from God and God's high standard of love and justice, separation from one another, and separation from our best selves. Therefore, all of us are sinners, and our sinfulness is the cause of much of the world's suffering. Separation, in whatever form, builds walls, erects barriers, and keeps God's will from flourishing. Separation does not lead to wholeness, unity, and peace. It is the fertile soil of suffering.

It is tempting to think of other people as sinful while not facing our own sinful nature. Understanding ourselves as sinful people deepens our faith and makes us kinder, more open to others, more humble, more positive and encouraging, and more realistic about life. When it comes to sinning, we seem to know more about others than we know about ourselves. There is, however, enough sin to go around; and no one, absolutely no one, is outside its grasp.

Sin is harmful to us. It prevents us from experiencing abundant life and threatens to destroy us. If we do not face and forgive sin, it grows bigger and bigger with the passing of time. As we saw in the previous chapter, it is important to remember that we are to have a forgiving and redemptive spirit when ministering to people who are suffering because of some sinful act they have committed. Those who represent Christ and the church must never forget that we are to be a redemptive community where persons can be forgiven and set free.

The Universe Has Freedom

Not all suffering can be blamed on the misuse of human freedom. Suffering also comes because there is a certain freedom in the universe. The upheavals of nature have contributed to massive and unbearable suffering. *Does God plan for nature to go on a rampage? Are natural disasters punishment for the dark side of our lives?* These are just some of the questions that bombard our thinking.

We will not find answers to these questions that will fully satisfy the deepest longings of our hearts. I have never been totally at peace with my own conclusions, but I continue to seek understanding. At this juncture of my life, however, there are a few things I have come to believe with confidence.

---

*The Danger of Becoming
Desensitized*

It can be easy to become desensitized to the pain and suffering that happens on the larger scale of massive destruction. The daily newspaper, television newscasts, and the Internet bombard us with one story after another about those who suffer because of nature's fury, often resulting in information overload. If we are not careful, we can become immune and shut down our empathetic feelings. As people of faith, we must remember that no one is a statistic and no one's suffering is insignificant. Each life is just as important as another. Guarding ourselves from becoming desensitized to the suffering of others helps us to remain responsive.

I believe the Creator has given birth to a world where different pushes and pulls are at work. We live in a world with great differences in natural phenomena, and these differences can "bump" into each other or "mesh together." When this occurs, the unpredictable is sure to happen. The creation is not programmed so that one aspect of nature never touches or influences another. On the contrary, these dissimilarities have a mysterious way of challenging and influencing one another. For example, it is said that the flapping of a butterfly's wing in Japan has the potential to contribute to a strong wind in Europe. When such interactions happen, change and turbulence and even mass destruction are possible; and if people live in the vicinity, they will be affected. We cannot stop these interactions in nature, nor can we always get out of the way of the outcomes.

The universe is not programmed to run smoothly. There is a freedom in creation, just as there is a freedom within the human species.

The Consequence of Freedom

I believe this freedom that God has given both to human beings and to the universe brings with it the potential for suffering. I do not believe that God *desires* us to suffer. The God who is displayed in Jesus has a tender desire that all of God's sons and daughters will be healthy in body, mind, and spirit. Rather, I must conclude that God allows suffering because God allows sin, which is the consequence of our misuse of God's gift of freedom. If God did not grant freedom, we would be like puppets, with God pulling the strings of our every thought and action.

God chose to give us the gift of freedom because of God's love for us. God loves us enough not to harness us to a predetermined natural order. If God is love and if we are to love one another, then we must be free to do so. Humans programmed to love would not be lovers. Being free to love God and neighbor is a great and good gift. This understanding of freedom that grows out of God's love for humankind can help to guide us as we attempt to be present to those who suffer.

The Freedom to Respond

Thankfully, our freedom makes it possible for us to respond to those who suffer. We can use our freedom to care for those who suffer by reaching out with the gifts of our presence and our compassion. Responding with compassion is a wise use of our freedom.

When reaching out to those who suffer, I have found it helpful to keep in mind the image of a shepherd. In so doing, we follow the example of Jesus who was seen as the Good Shepherd.

Both the Hebrew Bible and the New Testament contain many references to shepherding. In that day, shepherding was not easy because the sheep had to be grazed in pastureland that did not have an abundance of grass and was rocky and hilly. Shepherding was an arduous and dangerous task because the sheep had to be led to good grazing, water, and shade. They had to be protected from wild beasts and robbers. The valleys could contain "shadows of death" (Psalm 23), and stray sheep had to be rejoined to the flock (Matthew 18:12). This is why it was important for the shepherd to have a "standing beside" quality.

Reaching out to those who are troubled due to impending death, suicide attempts, loss, grief, illness, emotional stress, or some other cause of suffering calls us to "stand beside" those who are suffering. Let's consider some of the ways we can stand beside those who suffer.

1. We stand beside those who suffer when we embody empathy. We can use our freedom to say something such as, "I'm sorry to hear that you are dealing with cancer" or "I am very sorry that your cancer has returned." Verbally expressing empathy can be a source of strength for those who suffer.

2. We stand beside those who suffer when we do not forget them. People who suffer are often cut off from friends, especially during long periods of recovery. A call, a card, an e-mail, or a brief visit can help them to feel remembered, especially on special days such as birthdays, anniversaries, and holidays.

3. We stand beside those who suffer when we offer specific help. "Let me know if I can help" is too general and vague. A suffering person is unlikely to take us up on that kind of offer. Consider offering to do things such as driving to appointments, babysitting, mowing the lawn, cleaning the house, calling doctors, updating a website, cooking a meal, or organizing friends to bring meals during the week. Shepherds are specific in the many ways that they care for the sheep.

4. We stand beside those who suffer when we continue to include them in fellowship activities. Invite them to dinners, sporting events, church functions, and office parties. They may not feel like participating, but it feels good to be invited. Shepherds include all of the sheep at the watering hole.

5. *We stand beside those who suffer when we truly listen to them.* People who suffer say that it is most meaningful to be heard—truly listened to—and understood. We do not need to relieve our own anxiety by leaping in with advice, chatter, or opinions. Suffering often robs people of control—over their bodies, their schedules, and their plans for the future. Active listening can be a source of comfort. Shepherds listen to the needs of the sheep. If a person does not want to share, it is important to back away. Be respectful of where a person is and what a person wants to say.

6. *We stand beside those who suffer when we shepherd them without preaching to them.* A friend of mine who lost her husband said to me, "I cannot count the number of times people said to me, 'God has a plan out of this,' or 'God took your husband for a reason.' " To put it bluntly, sometimes people are ticked off with God because of the suffering that has come. Good shepherds lead, practice tenderness, and nourish without pontificating. Loving the sufferer as God loves them is often the best approach. Shepherds love their sheep, and so should we.

7. We stand beside those who suffer when we do not trivialize all that is happening. Saying that "everything is going to be OK" is not always helpful. Such sayings do not take the situation seriously. It is better to be a good listener than to offer wishful advice. Good shepherds know that the sheep are not always going to be OK.

Ways We Can Stand Beside Those Who Suffer

1. We stand beside those who suffer when we embody empathy.
2. We stand beside those who suffer when we do not forget them.
3. We stand beside those who suffer when we offer specific help.
4. We stand beside those who suffer when we continue to include them in fellowship activities.

---

5. We stand beside those who suffer when we truly listen to them.
6. We stand beside those who suffer when we shepherd them without preaching to them.
7. We stand beside those who suffer when we do not trivialize all that is happening.

In all of these ways, we can use our freedom to express tenderness toward the weak and wounded (Isaiah 40:11; Ezekiel 34:12). We are not physicians of the soul who dispense medication. Rather, our tenderness can be expressed through our vulnerability, which can be a medium for God's healing grace. One day Jesus asked Peter to "feed [his] lambs" (John 21:15) as proof of his love. This is the way of the servant. It is not a triumphant or manipulative approach. It is the way of the good shepherd who chooses to wisely use his or her freedom to care for troubled sheep.

Let us not forget that suffering has power. It can do a lot to the body, mind, and spirit. It holds the possibility of wrecking a person's life, cracking confidence, and breaking the soul; and it can leave the sufferer wasted and torn asunder. Like a bandit, it can steal a person's voice, self-image, and health. It can cause a person to know the difference between simply being tired and true fatigue, and it can cover with despair like a blanket. It even has the power to cause one to question faith in a loving God.

But there is a disease more devastating than suffering. It is hopelessness. There are no pills, vaccines, or treatments that can erase hopelessness. Those who suffer from lack of hope need people of faith who will say, "I will walk through this hell with you—no matter what. By embodying the love of Christ, I will show you the kind of love that cannot be destroyed by either suffering or death." By our compassionate presence, we will offer hope in ways we cannot understand. When we reach out to others, we must remember and truly believe that the living Christ goes before us. By our presence, we will witness to the Christ who is already present.

It is my hope that the practical resources given throughout the book and in the following index will be helpful to you as you practice the presence of the Great Physician.

SCRIPTURE
INDEX

Ecclesiastes 3:1-11

For everything there is a season, and a time for every matter under heaven:

> a time to be born, and a time to die;
> a time to plant, and a time to pluck up what is planted;
> a time to kill, and a time to heal;
> a time to break down, and a time to build up;
> a time to weep, and a time to laugh;
> a time to mourn, and a time to dance;
> a time to throw away stones, and a time to gather stones together;
> a time to embrace, and a time to refrain from embracing;
> a time to seek, and a time to lose;
> a time to keep, and a time to throw away;
> a time to tear, and a time to sew;
> a time to keep silence, and a time to speak;
> a time to love, and a time to hate;
> a time for war, and a time for peace.

What gain have the workers from their toil? I have seen the business that God has given to everyone to be busy with. He has made everything suitable for its time; moreover, he has put a sense of past and future into their minds, yet they cannot find out what God has done from the beginning to the end.

Psalm 23

A Psalm of David.
> The LORD is my shepherd, I shall not want.
> > He makes me lie down in green pastures;
> he leads me beside still waters;
> > he restores my soul.
> He leads me in right paths
> > for his name's sake.

> Even though I walk through the darkest valley,
> > I fear no evil;
> for you are with me;
> > your rod and your staff—
> > they comfort me.

> You prepare a table before me
> > in the presence of my enemies;
> you anoint my head with oil;
> > my cup overflows.
> Surely goodness and mercy shall follow me
> > all the days of my life,
> and I shall dwell in the house of the LORD
> > my whole life long.

Psalm 41:1-4

To the leader. A Psalm of David.
> Happy are those who consider the poor;

the LORD delivers them in the day of trouble.
The LORD protects them and keeps them
   alive;
   they are called happy in the land.
   You do not give them up to the will of their
   enemies.
The LORD sustains them on their sickbed;
   in their illness you heal all their infirmities.

As for me, I said, "O LORD, be gracious to me;
   heal me, for I have sinned against you."

Psalm 42:9-11

I say to God, my rock,
   "Why have you forgotten me?
Why must I walk about mournfully
   because the enemy oppresses me?"
As with a deadly wound in my body,
   my adversaries taunt me,
while they say to me continually,
   "Where is your God?"

Why are you cast down, O my soul,
   and why are you disquieted within me?
Hope in God; for I shall again praise him,
   my help and my God.

Psalm 51:1-12

To the leader. A Psalm of David, when the prophet Nathan came to him, after he had gone in to Bathsheba.

Have mercy on me, O God,
   according to your steadfast love;
according to your abundant mercy
   blot out my transgressions.
Wash me thoroughly from my iniquity,
   and cleanse me from my sin.
For I know my transgressions,
   and my sin is ever before me.
Against you, you alone, have I sinned,
   and done what is evil in your sight,
so that you are justified in your sentence
   and blameless when you pass judgment.
Indeed, I was born guilty,
   a sinner when my mother conceived me.

You desire truth in the inward being;
   therefore teach me wisdom in my secret heart.
Purge me with hyssop, and I shall be clean;
   wash me, and I shall be whiter than snow.
Let me hear joy and gladness;
   let the bones that you have crushed rejoice.
Hide your face from my sins,
   and blot out all my iniquities.

Create in me a clean heart, O God,
and put a new and right spirit within me.
Do not cast me away from your presence,
and do not take your holy spirit from me.
Restore to me the joy of your salvation,
and sustain in me a willing spirit.

Isaiah 26:3-4

Those of steadfast mind you keep in peace—
in peace because they trust in you.
Trust in the LORD forever,
for in the LORD GOD
you have an everlasting rock.

Matthew 5:1-12

When Jesus saw the crowds, he went up the mountain; and after he sat down, his disciples came to him. Then he began to speak, and taught them, saying:

"Blessed are the poor in spirit, for theirs is the kingdom of heaven.
"Blessed are those who mourn, for they will be comforted.

"Blessed are the meek, for they will inherit the earth.

"Blessed are those who hunger and thirst for righteousness, for they will be filled.

"Blessed are the merciful, for they will receive mercy.

"Blessed are the pure in heart, for they will see God.

"Blessed are the peacemakers, for they will be called children of God.

"Blessed are those who are persecuted for righteousness' sake, for theirs is the kingdom of heaven.

"Blessed are you when people revile you and persecute you and utter all kinds of evil against you falsely on my account. Rejoice and be glad, for your reward is great in heaven, for in the same way they persecuted the prophets who were before you."

John 3:16-17

For God so loved the world that he gave his only Son, so that everyone who believes in him may not perish but may have eternal life. Indeed, God did not send the Son into the world to condemn the world, but in order that the world might be saved through him.

Romans 8:31-39

What then are we to say about these things? If God is for us, who is against us? He who did not withhold his own Son, but gave him up for all of us, will he not with him also give us everything else? Who will bring any charge against God's elect? It is God who justifies. Who is to condemn? It is Christ Jesus, who died, yes, who was raised, who is at the right hand of God, who indeed intercedes for us. Who will separate us from the love of Christ? Will hardship, or distress, or persecution, or famine, or nakedness, or peril, or sword? As it is written,

> "For your sake we are being killed all long;
> we are accounted as sheep to be slaughtered."

No, in all these things we are more than conquerors through him who loved us. For I am convinced that neither death, nor life, nor angels, nor rulers, nor things present, nor things to come, nor powers, nor height, nor depth, nor anything else in all creation, will be able to separate us from the love of God in Christ Jesus our Lord.

2 Corinthians 1:3-5

Blessed be the God and Father of our Lord Jesus Christ, the Father of mercies and the God of all consolation, who consoles us in all our affliction, so that we may be able to console those who are in any affliction with the consolation with which we ourselves are consoled by God. For just as the sufferings of Christ are abundant for us, so also our consolation is abundant through Christ.

Hebrews 12:1-2

Therefore, since we are surrounded by so great a cloud of witnesses, let us also lay aside every weight and the sin that clings so closely, and let us run with perseverance the race that is set before us, looking to Jesus the pioneer and perfecter of our faith, who for the sake of the joy that was set before him endured the cross, disregarding its shame, and has taken his seat at the right hand of the throne of God.

James 5:13-16

Are any among you suffering? They should pray. Are any cheerful? They should sing songs of praise. Are any among you sick? They should call for the elders of the church and have them pray over them, anointing them with oil in the name of the Lord. The prayer of faith will save the sick, and the Lord will raise them up; and anyone who has committed sins will be forgiven. Therefore confess your sins to one another, and pray for one another, so that you may be healed. The prayer of the righteous is powerful and effective.

Revelation 21:1-4

Then I saw a new heaven and a new earth; for the first heaven and the first earth had passed away, and the sea was no more. And I saw the holy city, the new Jerusalem, coming down out of heaven from God, prepared as a bride adorned for her husband. And I heard a loud voice from the throne saying,

> "See, the home of God is among mortals.
> He will dwell with them;
> they will be his peoples,
> and God himself will be with them;
> he will wipe every tear from their eyes.
> Death will be no more;
> mourning and crying and pain will be no more,
> for the first things have passed away."

Other texts:

Suffering has the strange power to unleash love. This happens in two ways. First, when we suffer, we are more in tune to the sufferings of others. . . . I have an instant connection with persons who have had similar experiences. I am also far more compassionate and supportive of those who have walked the same path. I am more intense and in tune with the suffering of others.

Secondly, the world of human suffering calls for another world: the world of unselfish human love. Some people answer that call and some do not, but the call is there. The one who is the good Samaritan will not, with indifference, pass by the suffering of another person. The good Samaritan has a helpful and powerful solidarity with those who suffer in either major or minor ways. The good Samaritan will sympathize, stop, and help anyone who has been robbed by suffering. Any desire to help is called "good Samaritan" work. The eloquence of the parable calls every individual to personally bear witness to love in the face of suffering.

No organization or institution can replace the human heart, human compassion, or human love.

—Joe E. Pennel, Jr.